You Can Draw Wild Animals

Introduction

This book is to help you to draw and paint wild animals and there are many different ways to do this. You can use the step-by-step drawing guides which encourage you to study the animal's size, shape and detail, and there are pages of animal drawings for you to copy. There are useful tips for drawing animals at the zoo and at the museum and ideas for sketchbook practice.
But the most important thing is to **enjoy drawing**.

Making a sketchbook

A great way to get better at drawing is to keep a sketchbook. All good artists do this. You can buy one or just as easily make one by clipping pieces of paper together. In either case, it is a good idea to prepare each double page by giving it a background. Look at the suggestions below. It is fun to draw on these surfaces and they will help you make really interesting drawings. (Notice that some of the drawings in this book use prepared backgrounds too.) Look for the symbol for sketchbook ideas.

tea

coffee

white paint

brown pa

grey

old packaging lightly painted over

pa of

Lions

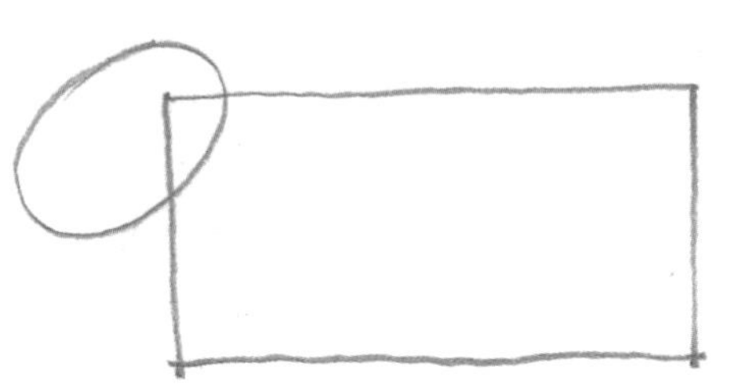

Observe

Look carefully at a lion. If you can't get to a zoo (see p.15), then look at this lion.

Key points

I usually begin with the eyes. Notice how drawing in the patches of white around the eyes really helps your drawing to look like a lion. Also the lines of black dots beneath the nose are important details.

Shape

The lion's body is roughly rectangular in shape so it might help if you sketch this in first.

Lions and tigers are members of the cat family. So if you look at and draw a cat, this will also help you to draw lions and tigers.

Colour

Almost half of my lion is covered by his shaggy mane which is made up of many different shades of yellow and brown – not just one colour.

Tip

Don't forget to draw the lion's ear, almost hidden in his mane.

Drawing tool

This lion is drawn with a 2B pencil. Pencil will give you many different shades and tones, from almost black to pale grey. The softer the pencil, the greater variety of tones.

Lion hunt!

Lions appear on many different products and packaging. Try recording these in a sketchbook. You can copy them or stick in pictures.

How many can you find?

The best way to produce a good drawing is to look carefully at the animal and try to draw what you see.

The shaggy mane goes as far as the front legs.

More Big Cats

The most important features of a tiger are its stripes and beautiful orange colour.
Look at the pattern made by the orange and white fur on the tiger's face and body.
If you can get this right it will make all the difference.
No two tigers have exactly the same pattern so look really carefully.

Here are two pages full of lions and tigers and other big cats.
Practise copying them. You could also try to draw them in a landscape.

☆ SPECIAL TIP!

The best practice of all is to draw animals from life, so this probably means a visit to the zoo (see p. 15).

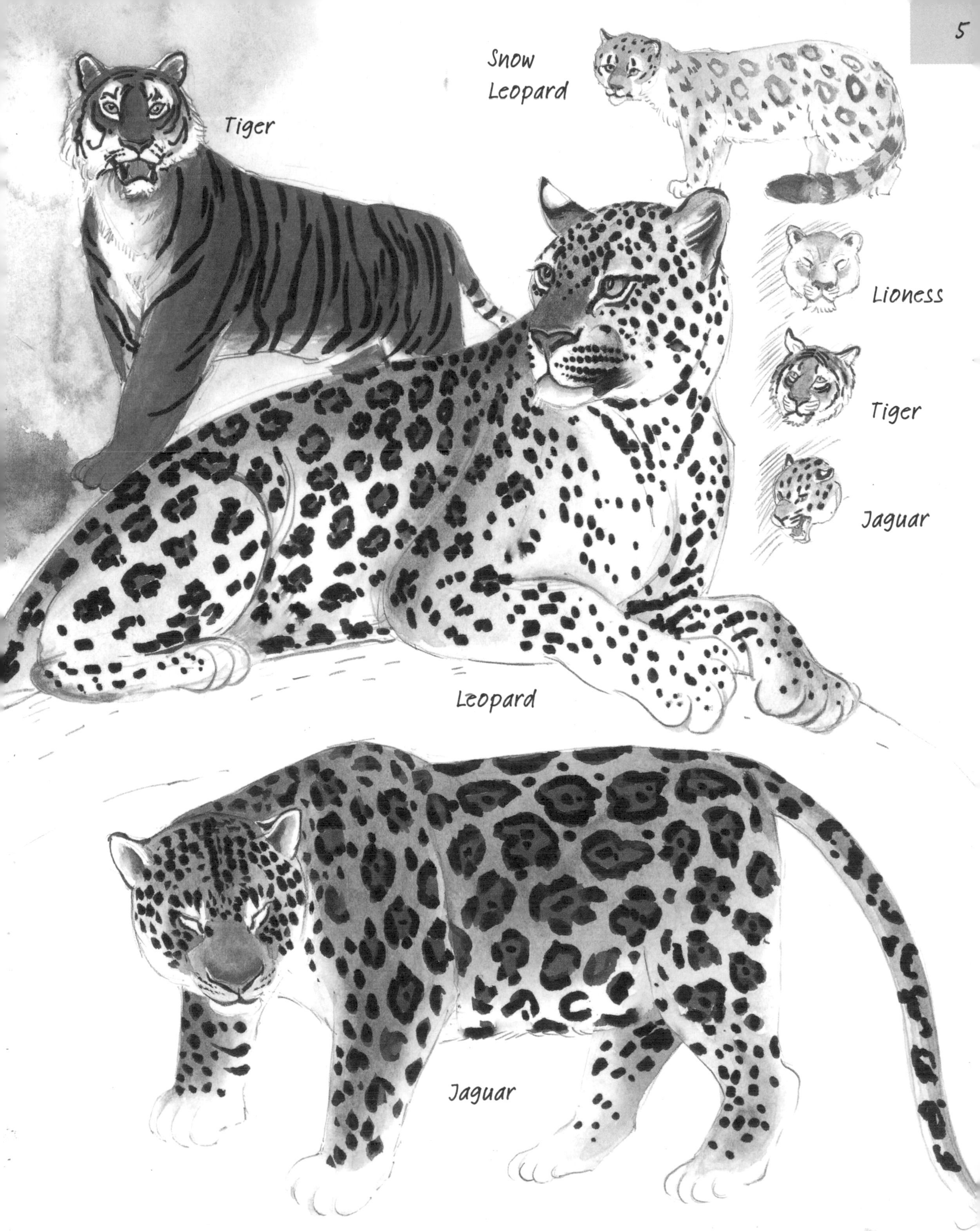

Notice how the jaguar is heavily built and has marks inside the spots, unlike the leopard.

Brown Bears

Shape

An oval will give you a shape for the body and the neck. The head is very roughly a rectangle.

Tip

Draw lightly to start with and gradually 'flesh out' your drawing adding the features.

Key point

Notice how the highest point is the Brown Bear's shoulder. This is very characteristic and will help make your drawing look right. Draw a line from the peak of the shoulder downwards to give you the position of the front paw.

Making your mark

Draw a series of squares in your sketchbook and practise filling in each with different marks. You could use a pencil, pen, brush, or chalk. The more varied the marks you make, the more you will increase your chance of producing a good drawing. Look at the range of pencil marks used to draw the Brown Bear's fur. Sketchbook exercises like this really improve your skill in handling materials.

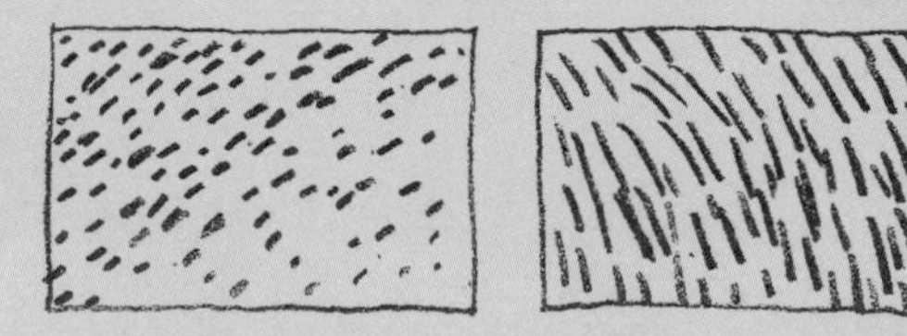

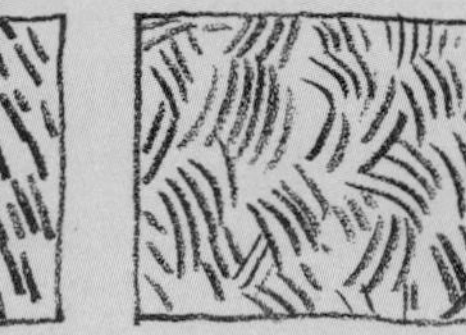

Observe

Notice how the shaggy fur helps to show the animal's form.

Drawing tool

All these bears are drawn with a 4B pencil. This gives a good range of tones for fur.

Polar Bears

These magnificent bears are now rarely seen in zoos, so you could draw them at a museum, or even from a video. This is a challenge, but great fun – and, as a last resort, there is always the pause button!

Fish

Fish in an aquarium are great fun to draw. They are constantly moving but you'll find that they often return to the same position so you have an excellent chance to draw them well.

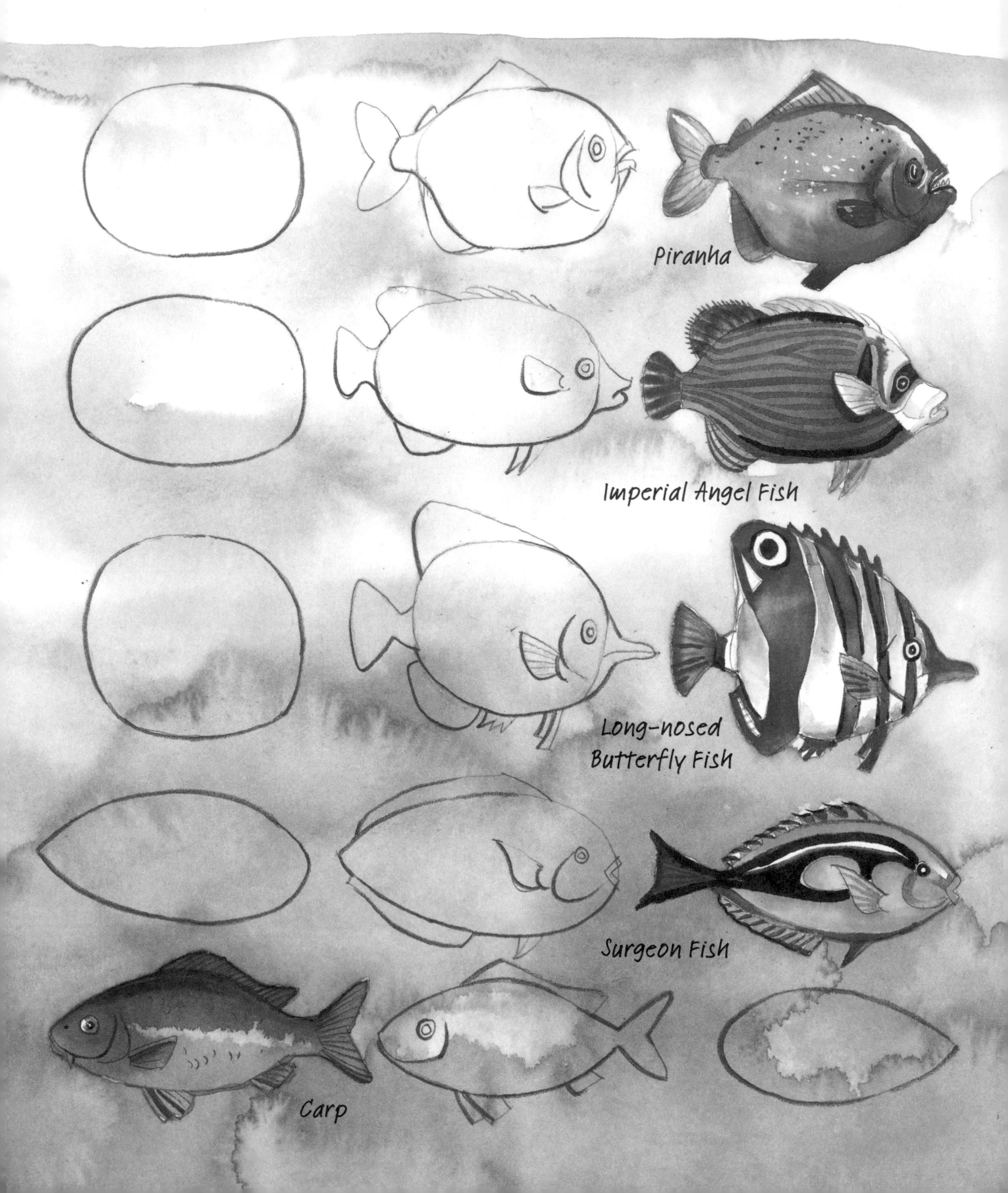

Observe

Look carefully at the fish. They may be different shapes and sizes but they all have gills, fins, two eyes and a tail.

Shape

Draw in the basic shape LIGHTLY. Add the fins, gill, tail, and the eye.

Colour

These fish are beautiful because of their varied colours and patterns. Enjoy adding these details.

Key point

Try to make your colours dazzle and sparkle as they do on the marine fish. Felt pens used with water are ideal (see Parrots, p. 12).

Tip

Be careful – some fish, like the Long-nosed Butterfly Fish, have a false eye to frighten enemies. Don't be fooled!

Drawing from life

A fishmonger gave me these fish heads, so I could make careful, detailed drawings of them. This is called 'observational drawing' and certainly helps you to draw better. Ask a grown-up to buy you a fish from a fish shop. Then you can try some observational drawings in your sketchbook. Remember, prepare your sketchbook first.

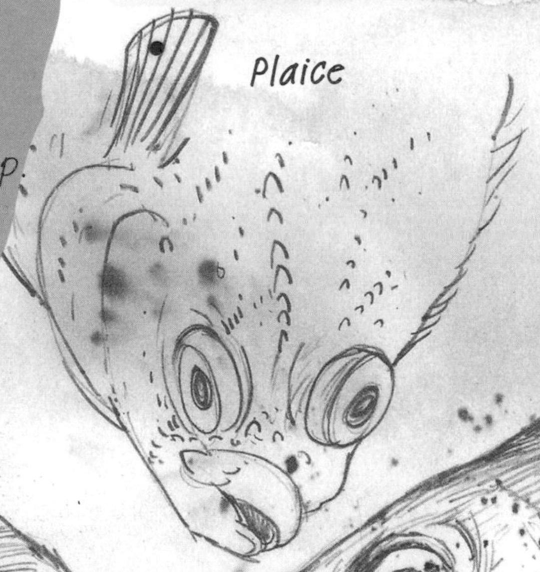

Plaice

Salmon

Mackerel

Drawing tool

This paper was prepared by washing it in coffee! You can also use watercolour for the bright fish. See p. 25.

Birds

Whether you live in the countryside or the town you will probably be surrounded by birds. Once you have mastered the basic shape, you should manage to draw any species and there are thousands to choose from.

If you put out scraps regularly for birds not too far from a window, you will have ready subjects to draw. You need to see clearly and be able to draw in comfort without disturbing the birds.

Eagle Owl

Shape

A small rectangle is a good base for the head. Make the sides of this rectangle bulge outward – this will help with the shape. Find the centre of the rectangle and this will give you a guide for the beak and eyes. A large oval is ideal for the body.

Falcon head

Key point

It is the markings on the Peregrine Falcon that really make this bird recognisable. Try practising the falcon's head and plumage (feathers) in your sketchbook.

Observe

Notice how adding the 'eyebrows' gives this falcon his angry bird-of-prey stare.

Tip

Draw as lightly as you can at first, then darken your pencil line when you are sure it is correct.

Mallard

Peregrine Falcon

On the spot

Try taking your sketchbook to a park where there are ducks. You'll find the ducks are used to people being around and so are quite tame. This kind of 'location' drawing is the best possible kind of practice. Look carefully at your subject and draw what you see.

Parrots

For the main shape of the parrot, use the step-by-step drawings in Birds, p. 10.

Drawing tool

Felt pens are great for bright, brilliant colour. So they are perfect for drawing these very colourful and noisy birds.

Puffin

Crossbill

African Grey Parrot

Use felt pens to colour small areas of the bird.

Then use a wet brush to spread the ink around and colour the whole bird.

Wait for the colour to dry and then add the final details with the felt pens.

Avocet

Tip

BE CAREFUL - don't use too much water, a little goes a long way.

Red and Blue Macaw

Spoonbill

Flamingo

Beak collection

There are many different types of birds with many different types of beaks, each adapted to suit the needs of its owner. Try drawing a collection of different beaks in your sketchbook.

* Only one bird out of the many thousands of species has a beak with the top half much shorter than the bottom half.

Can you see it here?

Long-billed Iiwi

Skimmer

The last colour I added to these toucans was black as it runs easily into the other colours and smudges them.

Keel-Billed Toucan

Red Breasted Toucan

Toco Toucan

Scarlet Macaw

Hyacinthine Macaws

Here are some tropical birds for you to copy.
Try to capture their bright and brilliant colours.
Use the technique described on the opposite page.

Elephants

Elephants are the largest living land animals but are surprisingly quiet. Notice how careful and precise their movements are. Try to capture this when you draw them.

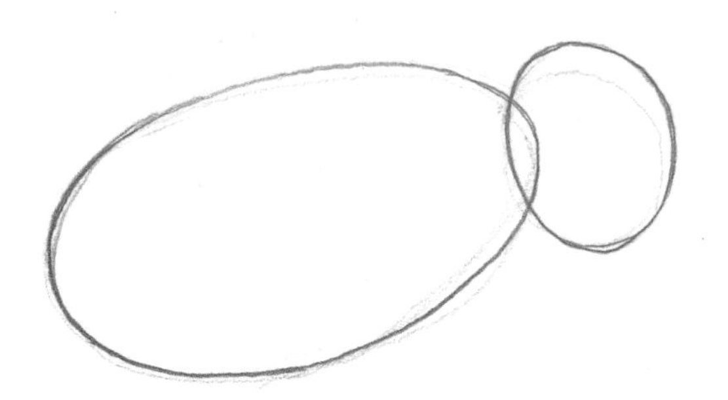

Observe

Look carefully at an elephant.

Shape

A large oval tilting downwards with a smaller circle at the top end will give you the basic shape. The trunk unfolded will reach to the ground. Look carefully at the bumps on the elephant's head. They are important and will help make your drawing convincing. As always, the key to success is looking and noticing.

Key Point

This is an Asiatic Elephant. It has smaller ears than its African cousin and an arched back. It also has four toenails on each back foot – an African elephant only has three.

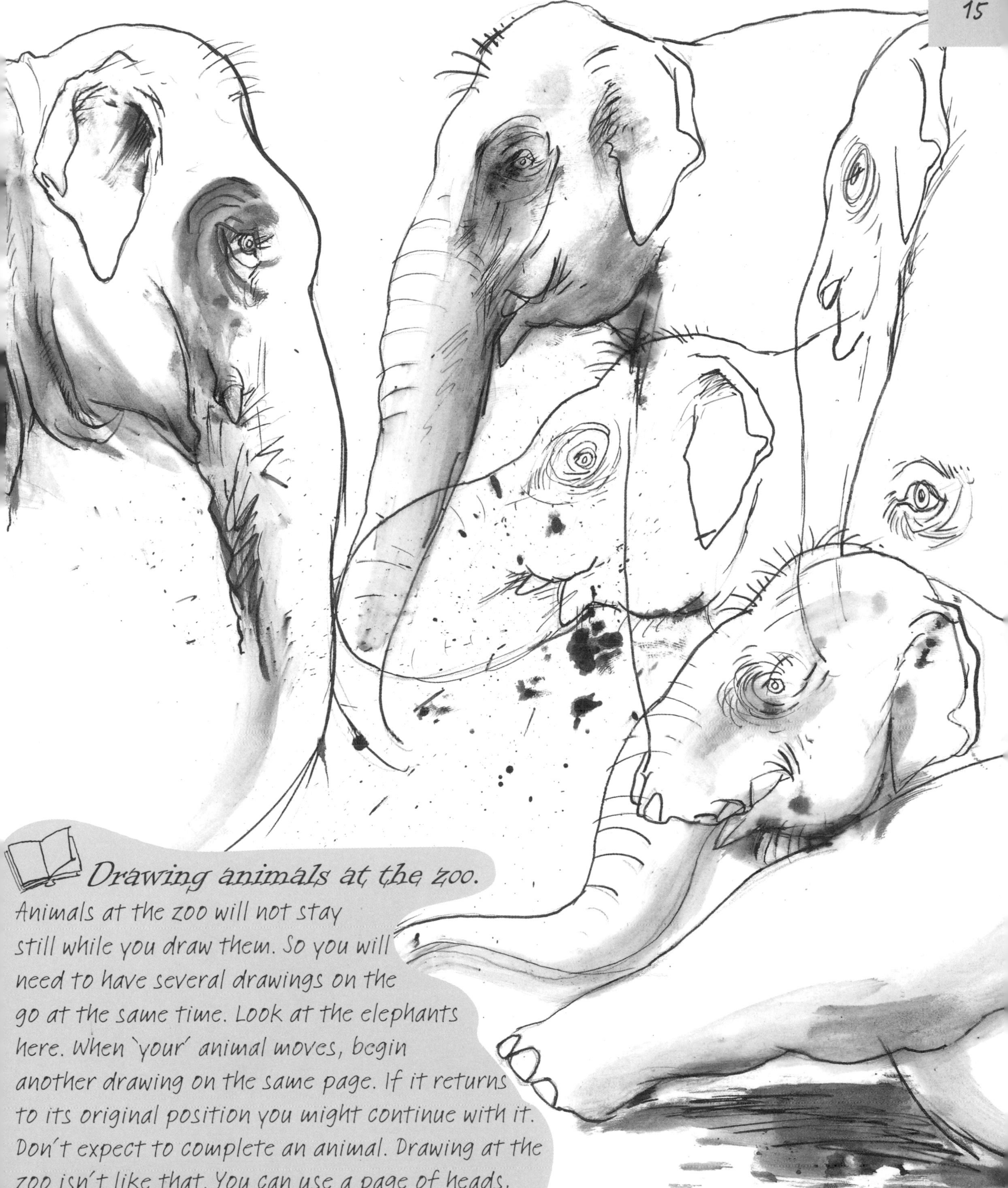

Drawing animals at the zoo.

Animals at the zoo will not stay still while you draw them. So you will need to have several drawings on the go at the same time. Look at the elephants here. When `your' animal moves, begin another drawing on the same page. If it returns to its original position you might continue with it. Don't expect to complete an animal. Drawing at the zoo isn't like that. You can use a page of heads, legs and bodies to construct a finished drawing later. That's how most artists work.

Deer and Antelope

These animals are graceful and very beautiful. Whatever their size, the basic shape is the same for any of the huge variety of species of antelope. The tiny Royal Antelope is no bigger than a rabbit, yet the Moose can be nearly 2.5 metres tall at the shoulder, taller than a very tall basketball player!

White-tail Deer

Springbok

Observe

Look at this White-tail Deer.

Shape

A rectangle for the body and a circle for the head will start you off. Remember – draw lightly at first and gradually strengthen your drawing when you are happy that it's accurate.

Key point

This White-tail Deer is leaping through the forest. Try to capture something of its energy and life in this pose. Your White-tail Deer should look as if it has leapt onto the page and may just leap off again. The quick pen drawings of Impala attempt to do just that.

Impala

Bongo

Topi

Brindle Gnu

Blackbuck

Dama Gazelle

Chital Deer

Head hunting

See how many species of deer and antelope you can find. Look in books, magazines, museums, zoos and parks and on the television. Then just sketch a collection of heads, like this.

Langur Monkeys

Monkeys are lively and often fast moving. This can make them difficult to draw from life.

Observe

Look at this Langur. Notice his long arms, legs and tail. He has five fingers and a thumb like us but they are long and thin.

Key point

The body is rather like an oval and the Langur's head in proportion is quite small and square (see detail on the opposite page). Noticing things like this will make all the difference to your drawing. Draw the arms, legs and tail in with lines first, then add the details.

Drawing tool

Try using a ball-point pen or a fountain pen. These are good tools for drawing quickly.

Langur head

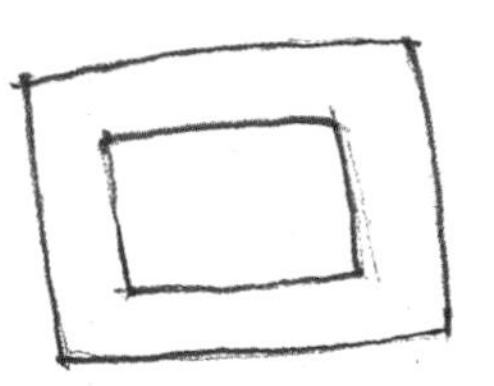

Shape

The Langur's face is square in shape and fringed with white fur. Try lightly drawing a square within a square to start you off. Then sketch in the shape of the face and the eyes, nose and mouth. Finally draw in the hair and shade in the darker face, ears and top of the head.

Tip

Notice how the eyes are heavily shaded by the Langur's brow.

Looks familiar

We have similar features to monkeys as you've probably noticed! So if you look in the mirror and draw your own face and hands in your sketchbook, this will help you to draw monkeys.

Langur

The Langur's fur is quite long and thick so add this at the end with your drawing tool.

More Apes and Monkeys

Here are some more members of the monkey family for you to copy. The colour of their faces and pattern of their fur vary tremendously across the huge variety of species BUT they all follow the same basic shape.

Print primates

These monkeys belong to the Guenon family, so they all have a similar shape although different species have different markings. Try making a simple print. You can cut a simple monkey shape out of a piece of lino, a potato, or a piece of card as I have done here. Using this as a stamp I filled in their markings and patterns when I visited a natural history museum. It makes an exciting identification chart. Use the same idea for other animal species.

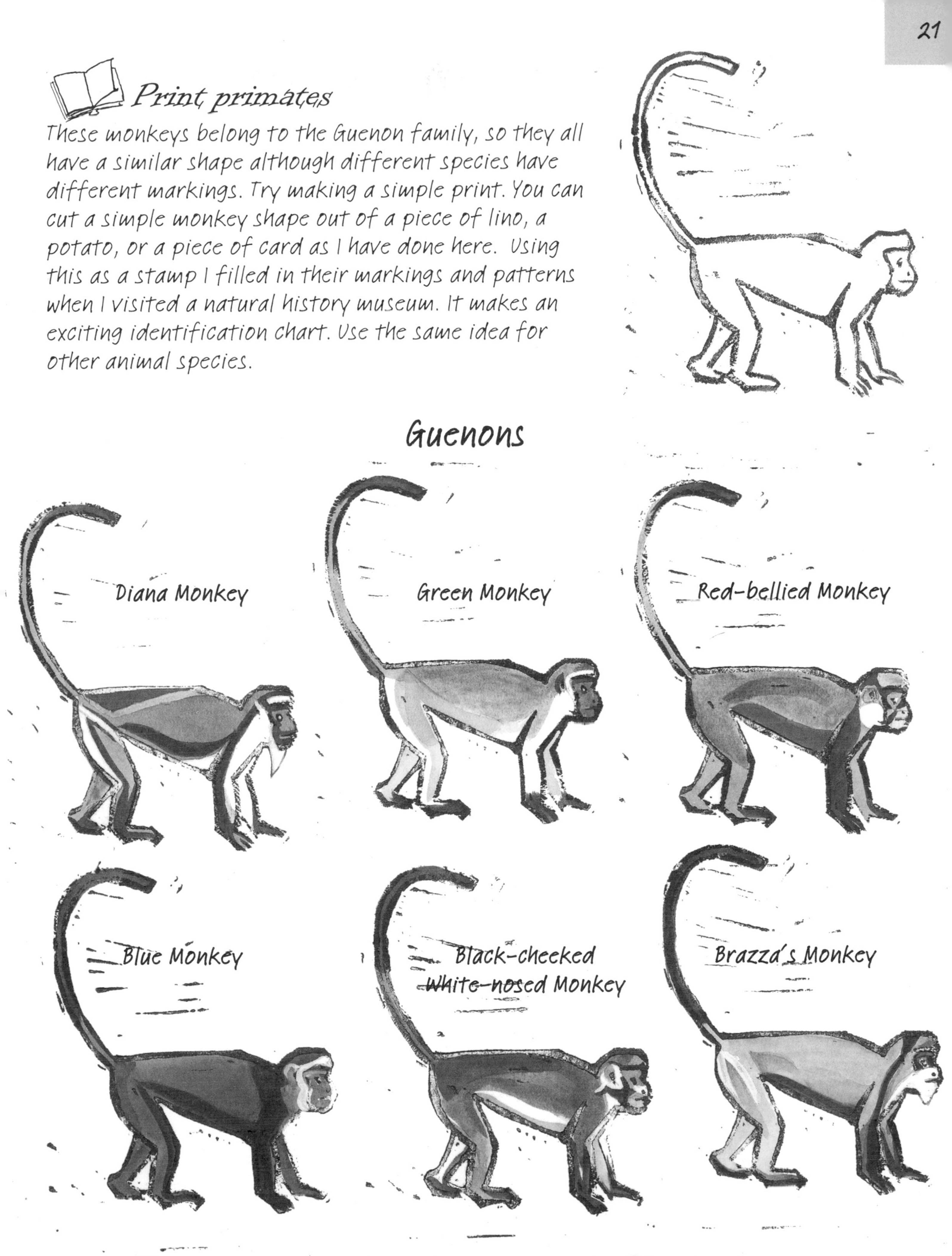

Reptiles and Amphibians

Reptiles often spend long periods without moving, especially if they are cold. So they are perfect subjects to draw from life. Even if they do move, they very often return to their original position so there really is the chance for a close look.

Observe

Like living dragons, iguanas are really members of the reptile family. Look at them carefully. They are lizards and share many similarities with geckos, skinks and even crocodiles.

Drawing tool

Here I have used a pencil but for the two iguanas at the bottom of page 23, I used a dip pen. It is the perfect tool for these spiky lizards.

Shape

An egg shape and a larger oval will give you the basic shape. The tail can be indicated with a line. This will ensure that all of your iguana fits on the page. A smaller egg shape inside the first one will give you a guide for the left eye. The bump of the right eye will be parallel. Draw in the flap of skin under the chin and the bump of the iguana's neck.

First sketch in the arms and legs and later 'flesh them out'.

The left hind leg is hidden in this drawing and we can only see the hand of the left arm.

Key point

The scales and spikes show the iguana's shape. The stripes running round the body and tail also help to make it look solid and three-dimensional. Notice how the stripes show the curve of the body – this is really important.

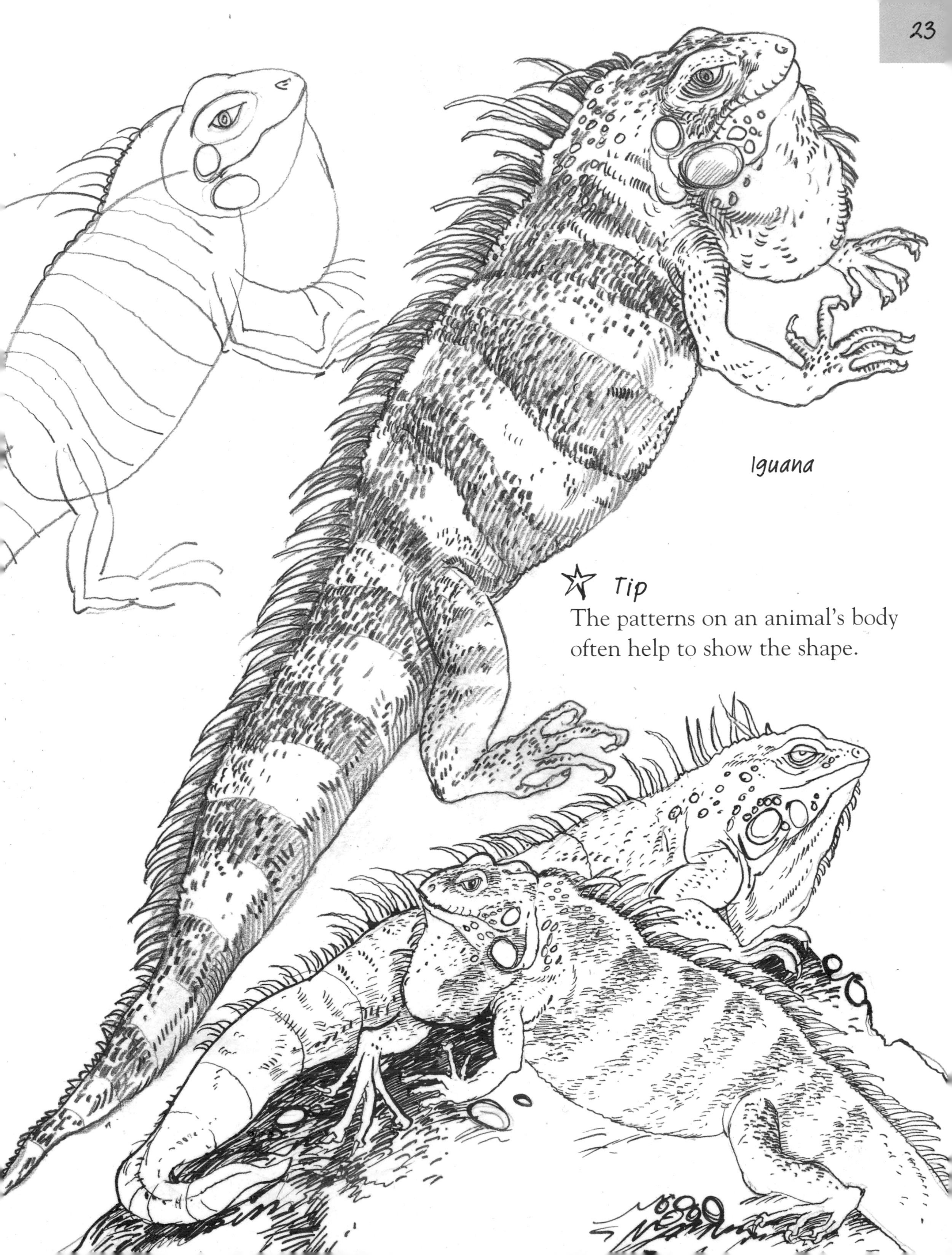

☆ *Tip*

The patterns on an animal's body often help to show the shape.

More Reptiles

Observe

The large bulging eyes and long arms and legs with spatula finger-tips are typical of all frogs.

Arrow-poison Frog (seven times larger than life!)

Mouth-breeder Frog

Drawing tool

Most of the frogs on this page are Arrow-poison Frogs. They have very bright colours, so use felt pen or watercolour (see opposite). I used colouring pencils for the Mouth-breeder Frog above. These are clean and easy to use but difficult to blend.

Reptile reference

Make a concertina of reptiles and amphibians to fold out of your sketchbook. Use pictures from magazines and newspapers. This is an excellent way to build up a store of reference ready to use at any time.

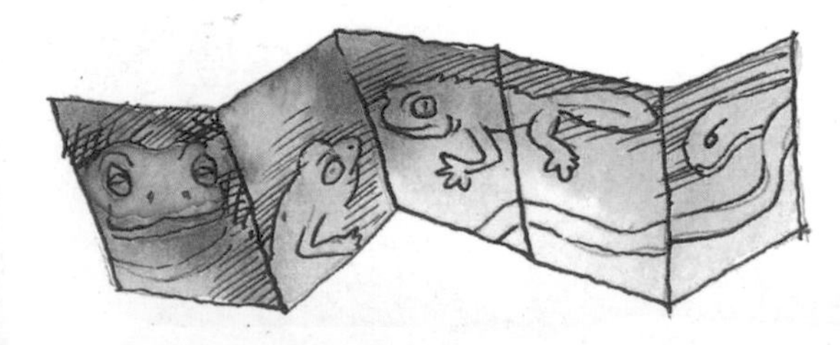

Here are lots of reptiles and amphibians for you to copy. This will be good practice when you draw them from life. Look at the similarities between them. Drawing one will help you to draw another.

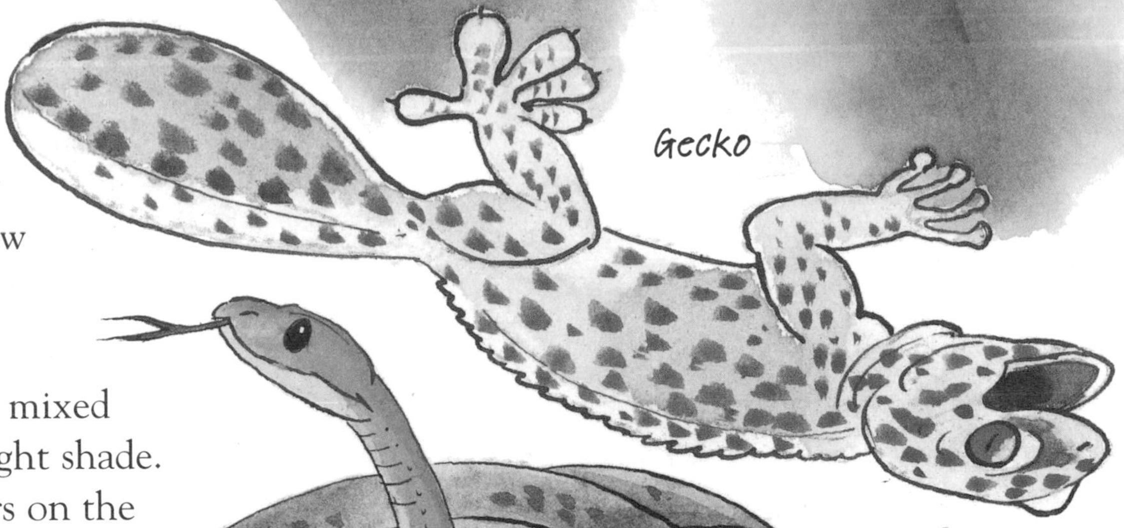

Gecko

Drawing tool

Watercolour can be mixed to get exactly the right shade. To blend the colours on the page, work quickly while the colour is wet.

Green Mamba

☆ Tip

Don't try to draw every scale on the snake. Use them to show the shape.

Camels and Zebras

Camels

Camels are curious animals to draw, with their strange legs and humps. They are good to draw from life as they usually move slowly.

Observe

Look at a camel carefully.

Shape

Try drawing an egg shape for the head and an oval for the body. The thick fur on the camel's neck makes it appear to bulge outwards. Draw this in. Gradually build up your drawing following the steps here.

Key point

Obviously the camel's humps are a vital feature. This is a Bactrian camel with two humps. The Arabian camel has one hump and is often wrongly called the Dromedary, which is in fact a special breed of one-humped camel used for riding.

Drawing tool

This finished drawing was made using a fountain pen. This is ideal for drawing on location. It doesn't dry up and can be smudged with water to show shadow.

Zebras

Observe

Look how the pattern of stripes on this zebra helps to show its shape.

Shape

Start by drawing an oval for the body and a smaller oval for the head. Remember to draw lightly at first. Gradually draw over these shapes, sketching in the form of the zebra.

Key point

Different species of zebra have different stripe patterns but, as a general rule, zebras from further north in Africa are more heavily striped than zebras from the south.

Tip

Draw in the stripes first before thickening them up.

Family matters

Remember that horses and zebras are very similar. A zebra gallops in exactly the same way as a horse. Try sketching ponies and you'll be well-prepared to draw zebras.

Lemurs

Aye-ayes

This strange and extremely rare animal is sometimes called 'The Witch's Cat' and it's easy to see why.

Observe

It has huge ears and eyes and a long bushy tail. But its strangest features are its very long, bony fingers, especially the middle finger which it uses to poke into holes looking for grubs.

Key point

The Aye-aye's tail is over three-fifths of its length, so leave enough room on your paper to fit it all in.

Shape

Build up your drawing from an oval and a triangle. Then work on the eyes and ears, its dominant features.

Animal notes

As one of the world's rarest mammals, the chance to draw this Aye-aye at London Zoo was wonderful. It was very dark in the Aye-aye house and the Aye-aye was constantly moving but you can learn a lot by just watching. Make written notes to jog your memory later. What does it do? Does it make a noise? How does it move?

Drawing tool

I used white acrylic to highlight the Aye-aye's long white hairs.

Ruffed Lemur

Black Lemur

Sifaka

Ring-tailed Lemur

Lemurs

Here are some other lemurs for you to copy. Try and find them at the zoo too.

Nocturnal Animals

Slow Loris

Bushbaby

Tarsier

Observe

These nocturnal animals are from different continents yet look how similar they are with their huge eyes, perfect for night-time vision.

Shape

Look at the Tarsier's head.
It is roughly rectangular in shape.
The body is a large oval.
Follow the step-by-step pictures on the opposite page to start you off.

Key point

The eyes are huge and quite close together so be especially careful when drawing them in – they must be right. In this drawing the Tarsier is gripping a tree so we can only see one arm and one leg. Draw them in. Don't forget the tail.

Drawing in the dark

*Try to draw something in a dark room.
Your eyes will gradually get used to the dark.
Later, try the same drawing again in full light.*

Drawing tool

As this animal is out and about at night, a dark background will give your drawing atmosphere. You can use chalk or white paint.

Draw a circle in the space where the oval and rectangle cross. This will be the Tarsier's nose and mouth.

Begin by drawing the rectangle and oval. Make the oval slightly overlap the rectangle.

Finally, finish your drawing by looking at the details. The Tarsier's fur, fingers and toe-nails, even the bark on the tree.

Bats

Bats are difficult to draw from life. They are fast moving, nocturnal mammals and almost impossible to see clearly.

Observe

The Bat's wing is really its arm. The four long fingers of the hand are open like a fan and provide a support for the skin.

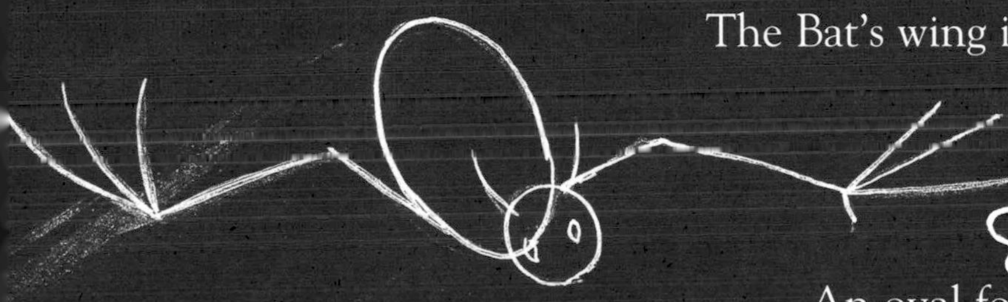

Shape

An oval for the body and a circle for the head will start you off. Then draw in the arms and fingers. Imagine the skin stretched over this frame.

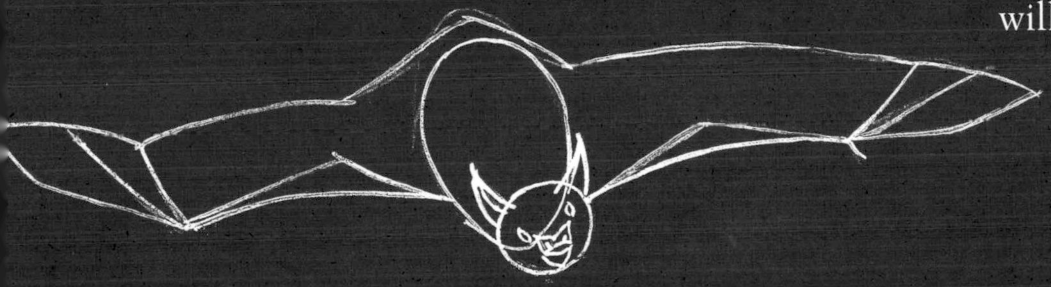

Top Ten Tips

- Try using lots of different implements to draw with.
- When you draw with a pencil, make sure it's sharp. Pencils range from H = hard to B = soft. An HB pencil is exactly in the middle. For drawing wild animals you will always need an HB or softer. Never draw with a propelling pencil.
- Use your eyes. Looking carefully at what you are drawing is essential.
- Try not to rub out too much.
- Practise and practise. The more you draw the better you will get.
- Drawing an animal from life is the best possible practice.
- Always carry your sketchbook with you – you never know when you might find something you want to draw.
- Keep all your drawings. If you look at them after a period of time you will see them in a new light. They can often look better than you thought.
- As well as drawing, make written notes. You can't draw the noise an animal makes but you can describe it.
- Most of all, enjoy your drawing!